FOREVER IN LOVE

forever in love

PUT A LITTLE FUN, EXCITEMENT,
AND ROMANCE BACK INTO YOUR
RELATIONSHIP!

ENCOURAGING NUGGETS, SWEET-NOTHING QUOTES,
LOVE-IN-ACTION CALENDAR CHALLENGE, AND
FOREVER IN LOVE MEMORY CARD GAME

VARINIA PEACE

Charleston, SC
www.PalmettoPublishing.com

Forever in Love
Copyright © 2006, 2020 (Second Edition) by Varinia Peace

Paperback ISBN: 978-1-64990-168-2
eBook ISBN: 978-1-64990-167-5

This book is dedicated to all the lovers out there. It is dedicated to the married, to the engaged, to those contemplating marriage, to the newlyweds, and to those who aren't even dating. Yes! There are encouraging and priceless nuggets in it for all! *Forever in Love* will inspire, encourage, and enlighten you of what it takes to experience a healthy and successful relationship. My hope and prayer is that couples value, appreciate, and cherish the love they have. Love doesn't come easy, and when you find a good thing, you should do your best to hold on to it!

CONTENTS

Author's Notes

MY MOTIVATION

God is my motivation in everything I do and in my everyday life. I am so grateful to him for blessing me with this wonderful opportunity to write and publish this book. He moved through my heart to use this platform to encourage and speak life and hope into others. He is my hope, my joy, and my peace!

My beautiful mama, Fannie, motivates me in so many ways. She has always told me (and she still does to this day) that I can do anything that I put my mind to, and she has always encouraged me to believe in myself. I get my strength from her and her example—how she always continues to press on, no matter what she is going through. She is a loving, strong, and amazing woman!

My wonderful dad, Randolph—we have so much in common. We share in the same interests and aspirations. I got my ability to sing, write, and teach and my creativity in general from him. We are always thinking about quotes and songs, and we are always bouncing ideas off of each other. He always encourages me in the word of God, and he encourages me to use my gifts and talents. He is an amazing dad!

Adrian, my amazing son, motivates me in countless ways. The life he lives is so inspiring, and his drive and commitment for his craft encourages me to stay hopeful and continue to pursue my dreams. He holds me accountable by giving me gentle reminders to stay focused and follow through. Thank you, Adrian, for your love, your wisdom, and the strength you give me.

SPECIAL THANKS

A special thanks to my dear and sweet friend Christine Sullivan. I would always ask her to look over my books because I knew she was a book scholar. This lady has read so many books, and she is so full of wisdom, imagination, and creativity—she was my go-to for advice. Thank you so much, Ms. Sullivan, for allowing me to bother you all the time with my book projects.

MY INSPIRATION

My heart for people, for marriages, and for couples inspired me to write *Forever in Love*. It actually started out many years ago as a book of "sweetheart quotes" for Valentine's Day. I will never forget. I was volunteering at a high school in 2012, the year of my son's graduation. My friend and I ended up doing a fundraiser for a special school project. It was the month of February, and with Valentine's Day just around the corner...an idea came immediately to my mind—Valentine Sweetheart Telegrams! I shared the idea with the committee, and it was a go! I came up with lots of sweetheart quotes; we printed them on nice paper, rolled them up like miniature scrolls with red ribbons, and sold the telegrams to the students for one buck. The students absolutely loved it! The fundraiser was a success! Then a few years later, those sweetheart telegrams became an idea for a book of sweetheart quotes for couples. Who knew that those sweetheart quotes would become *Forever in Love!*

Forever in Love is a book filled with sweet nuggets of encouragement and hope for all marriages. It is intended to encourage couples to embrace and to cherish the love they have. As I began to write *Forever in Love*, I realized that there is something in it for all couples, whether married, engaged, or contemplating marriage—and even for those who are single!

Many people are still wishing, hoping, and praying for that special someone. Let me just say, if you have a good thing, you should do your best to "hold on to it." Whatever problems or challenges you may face; it's worth working it out—no matter what the cost. I say, give it your all, and then some, and then a little bit more, before you decide to call it quits. It is always easy to take the easy way out, but it takes heart, determination, and commitment to stand and fight! No matter what you are going through, I encourage you to stay, stick, and stand together and fight for that special thing that you have been blessed with. I am reminded of a saying that goes, "Anything that is worth having is worth fighting for." As for you who are still waiting on that special someone—keep hope alive; love is on the horizon!

Introduction

Before you read any farther, allow me to make this disclaimer: I do not claim to be a "love doctor," so please spare me the name *Dr. Love*. However, I do understand what it takes to have a healthy and successful relationship. You may think it strange coming from someone who is divorced, but experience is a good teacher! After almost twenty years of marriage, I have not only been through a lot and experienced a lot, but I have also learned a lot. You see, I know that it takes true love, trust, and respect, accompanied with the three *Cs*—communication, commitment, and compromise—as well as a good dose of humor, to have a strong and healthy relationship. These things are essential to fostering a love that will last forever!

When you are in a relationship with someone, you shouldn't feel like you are alone. If there seems to be some distance between you and your significant other, if you are feeling alone and by yourself, if you feel like something is missing or something is broken, and even if you feel like your relationship has gotten boring or stale—it is time for you and your significant other to have a serious talk. But have no fear; everything in your relationship can be restored, and your love can be reignited! All it takes is your willingness to communicate with each other and work together. Consider your-selves a partnership or a team; as we all know, there is no *I* in team! It takes two people equally giving it their all in a relationship. You must keep doing those things you used to do to keep your love alive, fresh, and new, but you MUST do it together!

Even in the midst of all the work—reaching your goals, pursu-ing your dreams, raising the children, etc.—you have to remem-ber that you have a partner. Don't get it twisted, and don't miss it. Working, paying the bills, putting food on the table, and pursuing your dreams are all important things, but you have to keep *the main thing,* the main thing: your relationship and your family!

I challenge you to take these simple nuggets to heart. I guarantee they will remind you of why you fell in love in the first place. We are going to touch on several important topics that are essential to hav-ing a strong and lasting relationship. I hope I can share something with you that will help your love life flourish in every way!

The Marriage Union

When God created marriage, he created a beautiful thing. It's the incredible beginning of a brand-new love story that you and your spouse get to write together. God specifically designed marriage for his purpose of companionship, intimacy, and having children. He designed this sacred union so that a man and a woman could live a fulfilled life together as partners, supporting each other as they raise a family together. This sacred union is a bond between you, your spouse, and God—a bond that cannot easily be broken.

Ecclesiastes 4:12: "Though one may be overpowered, two can defend themselves. A cord of three strands is not quickly broken." No matter what challenges you face in life or in your marriage, if God is the center, you can and will overcome.

The scriptures tell us that what God put together let not man separate (Matthew 19:6). When your marriage is God-breathed, then it was meant to be, and it is meant to work. Both of you just have to be willing to make it work. When we understand God's intention for marriage, we will enter into that marriage union with the understanding that it is intended to last forever. Marriage should not to be taken lightly, but often times it is. Making a commitment to marry someone is a serious step. The vows that we take before God and others—for better or for worse, for richer or poorer, in sickness and in health, to love and to cherish, till death do us part, according to God's holy ordinance; thereto I pledge myself to you—these marriage vows should be taken seriously and spoken from a sincere heart.

When we choose to put God first in our lives, we will choose to put him first in our marriage. He will guide us in how we are to love and treat each other. God's love is the key. There are many encouraging and uplifting scriptures about how a man should love and treat his wife and how a wife should love and treat her husband.

Ephesians 5:25: "For husbands, this means love your wives, just as Christ loved the church. He gave up his life for her." This doesn't mean that a husband has to lay down his life for his wife. This means that he lives to serve his wife, and he places her first; making her top priority. A husband loves and respects his wife, and he sees to it that all her needs are met. God gave husbands the role of leadership in a marriage to lead and guide his wife and family in the way of Christ. A husband should always seek God for spiritual counsel; not only for himself, but for his wife and family as well.

Ephesians 5:22-23: "Wives, submit to your own husbands, as you do to the Lord. For the husband is the head of the wife as Christ is the head of the church, his body, of which he is the Savior." This means that wives honor and respect their husbands and their leadership role in their marriage. They respect their husbands as the spiritual leader of the family. In doing this, the wife is honoring God and trusting her husband to lead her and the family according to God's perfect guidance.

God's love is the greatest love of all, and his love will lead and guide you in your life and on your journey of love and marriage. I

4

encourage you to stay committed to God, to your faith, and to each other so you can have a fulfilling and successful marriage. Pray, read, and study the scriptures together. Encourage and support each other in the word of God daily, and this will be a sure foundation for your love to grow strong and stay healthy. You know the saying: "A family that prays together stays together."

Get Back to Each Other

Have you stopped *wooing and wowing* each other? Are you wondering why? Could it be because you have stopped doing the things you use to do that kept your relationship fun *and exciting? So* often, I hear people say (when asked why they split up), "We just grew apart" or "We fell out of love." Well, I say it's because you just stopped. You stopped communicating w*ith eac*h other, you stopped speaking each other's love language, and you stopped doing those things together that really mattered. Those sweet and special things that kept you close, like going out to dinner, going to the movies, or going on long walks in the park together. You see, often times when we settle down with each other, we can get so comfortable that *we just stop*. But to keep your love alive, you must continue doing those special things that mean so much!

If these essential things cease, eventually you will find yourself growing apart. I have often heard that, after you decide to settle down and tie the knot, all the romance, fun and, excitement comes to an end. But it doesn't have to be that way! Once you settle down, it shouldn't be the end of your relationship, but the beginning of your life-long adventure. You both have a part to play in keeping your love alive!

MEN

When you first met your woman, you were the happiest man in the world, and you vowed to make her the happiest woman in the world. When you first met her, you wined and dined her, you sent her flowers on every special occasion or just because, and you bought her countless boxes of chocolates and even pulled out her chair before she sat down to eat. Talk about those chivalrous days! Now, those romantic and spontaneous dates, those beautiful flowers, those cute little love notes, those thoughtful and *just-because* gifts, and those sweet promises have all ceased.

Your woman not only longs for your attention and affection, but she needs it. Not to be validated, but to feel loved and appreciated. When was the last time you spent some time with your woman or took her out on a romantic date? When was the last time you paid her a compliment? Let me tell you, it makes her day when you pay her a compliment or notice something new or different about her (e.g., her new hairdo; her nails; a new dress, a new pair of shoes; and, yes, even that new red lipstick!). Your woman wants to hear that she looks good in those distressed jeans; she wants to hear you say, "Baby, your hair is beautiful today." When you notice things like this about your woman, it's like food to her soul! My encouragement to you is to get back to those sweet and simple things that kept your woman happy, satisfied, and feeling like she is the most important woman on the face of this earth! In other words, keep her top priority!

WOMEN

When you first met your man, you were the happiest woman in the world, and you vowed to make him the happiest man in the world! This man swept you off your feet! You were determined to make him happy and keep him satisfied! You kept your makeup flawless, your hair perfectly styled, and you were dressed to impress. But your beauty and style weren't the only things that attracted your man to you. Your man was attracted to that ambitious woman too. You were a dreamer with goals that you were determined to reach. But perhaps you have gotten so comfortable that you have stopped dreaming.

Now, your man is wondering what happened to that driven and ambitious woman he once knew. Ladies, we should never get so comfortable that we lose ourselves in our relationship or stop pursuing our dreams. Your man was blown away by your strength, how you took pride in yourself, your drive and determination. He saw success in you, and he wants for you to be successful. I encourage you to stay true to yourself. Get back to you and all the things you desired to do. And get back to doing those things that kept your man happy and satisfied!

Your man will probably never admit, but he needs attention and affection too. As women, we sometimes assume all the attention and affection belongs to only us. But our men need attention and affection too! Yes, a man needs to feel loved and appreciated; he needs to feel valued and needed. You have no idea what it does to a man's ego when you tell him how proud you are of him and how much you appreciate him. Compliments go a long way with a man as well. Try paying him a compliment and see what it does to his ego. A simple compliment can boost his ego so high that you have him singing his favorite song in the rain! Men love it when you tell them, "Baby, you are looking so good in those jeans." What's more, men also love it when you are flirtatious! So, get your flirt on!

It takes both of you to keep that romance light on! Yes, it takes some time and work, but both of you have to equally put in the work to make your relationship work. I understand that your jobs or careers can be quiet demanding, things will happen that are out of your control, and you may face many challenges along the way. But don't allow work or those challenges to get in the way of your beautiful and budding relationship. To keep your relationship fun and exciting, you have to find *twenty-one* fun and creative ways to keep each other interested, happy, and satisfied! I encourage you to *get back to each other*! Keep on reading; I want to talk about this *love thing* first!

True Love: It Never Fails

When I was sixteen years old, I dreamed of falling in love, getting married, and settling down for the rest of my life. I guess I always had a much older spirit, and people often told me that I was very mature for my age. I didn't care for dating and *shopping around* (if you know what I mean). I just wanted to find that special person, fall in love, and settle down. I believed that, when I met him, I would know that he was the right one for me. You will know when you have found that special someone. You will find yourself saying that he/she is *The One* and there is absolutely no doubt in your mind that you are meant to be.

In my past relationship, I was often told that love hurts. But in my heart, I knew different. You see, love doesn't hurt, but hurting people hurt others. They hurt from past hurts, guilt, shame, and regrets, from past relationships or something they may be struggling with personally. They continue living in that hurt because they have never dealt with it. They carry it with them everywhere they go, which means, unfortunately, they carry it into their relationships. That is why so many people are confused about what true love really is. They become victims of hurting people. It makes one ask the question "Is this really love?"

I believe that is why many people nowadays are deciding not to marry. Marriage is a beautiful thing, but some opt out because they are afraid of being hurt. You see, someone told them that they loved them, but all they ever experienced in their relationship was hurt. So, they put their guard up and vowed to never get hurt again. Despite what you have been through in your past relationships or what you believe concerning love, true love does not hurt. You may have never experienced true love before, or perhaps you have experienced bits and pieces of what true love really is. But true love does not hurt, and it never fails.

The kind of love that never fails is that I Corinthians 13:4-8 kind of love:

"Love is patient, love is kind. It does not envy, it does not boast, it is not proud. It does not dishonor others, it is not self-seeking, it is not easily angered, it keeps no record of wrongs. Love does not delight in evil but rejoices with the truth. It always protects, always trusts, always hopes, always perseveres. Love never fails."

This is true love; this is God's love, and when your relationship is built on God's love, it will not fail. When you put God at the center of your relationship, you can and will experience true and lasting love. Love is an action word, and you have to learn to put your love into action. It's more than just saying, "I love you"; it's your actions, your behavior, and your attitude toward the recipient of your love. There are many important ingredients in the recipe of love, but I would have to say the top three are trust, respect, and commitment.

Making a commitment is a huge step, just like marriage. When you commit to each other, you must know what you want individually and collectively. You establish your expectations, never compromising your happiness or who you are, and you work on building a life together, adhering to those expectations. When you love someone, you speak openly and honestly to each other; you listen to each other and value each other's feelings and needs. Give each other space; support each other's interests, hobbies, and careers and always build each other up. That's a love that will guarantee the life of your relationship!

When it comes to the recipe of love, there are more essential ingredients. Yes, there is always more! There is honesty, understanding, patience, communication, happiness, joy, intimacy, and forgiveness. Forgiveness is another extremely important ingredient in your love recipe!

Remember that love forgives. Unforgiveness is one of the many causes of divorces and breakups. Beautiful relationships are destroyed because of unforgiveness. You do not want to carry the burden of unforgiveness in your heart. Unforgiveness builds walls of anger, resentment, and bitterness. Unforgiveness steals so much of your precious time and joy. It brings unwanted stress, anxiety, and even depression. You must learn to forgive each other and move forward. Rehashing the past can only keep you walking in bitterness as you find yourselves caught up in constant arguments. It is imperative that you learn to forgive each other in order to have a healthy and lasting relationship. If forgiveness is something you have to put into practice, then I say, put it into practice! Forgiveness has to be a part of your everyday life, and it has to come straight from the heart!

In relationships, you will have misunderstandings and disagreements. This doesn't mean that you don't love each other; it just means that you are human, you have feelings and the bottom line- this is normal. It is normal to have arguments and disagreements. I believe that we get it in our minds that true love is supposed to be perfect, and if it isn't perfect, then, it isn't true love at all. But being in love does not exempt you from having problems or facing challenges in your relationship. Challenges will show up, but the important thing is to face those challenges head-on together.

SPECIAL NOTE

Whenever you are angry or upset, learn to give each other some time and space. We all know that it never works to try and discuss things when you are both upset. Setting aside time to take a deep breath and cool down can make all the difference in the world.

Anger and frustration can lead you to make some unhealthy decisions or choices. So be careful how you channel that anger and frustration. Do not allow yourself to make choices that you'll regret later. It is always good to cool off in a safe and healthy environment. I stress *safe and healthy* environment for these reasons. You see, often times we can get angry, and put ourselves in some bad situations. Going to a bar and getting wasted (if you indulge) is a bad idea. Going to the home of a negative friend or family member is a bad idea. Going to the home of a friend who is of the opposite sex is the worst idea. A friend of the *opposite sex is definitely the wrong place to end up.* Next thing you know, you'll find yourself explaining to your significant other that…one thing just led to another. You do not want to have that kind of conversation with your significant other. These escapes can only lead to bigger problems.

A WORD OF ADVICE

Go to a quiet and safe place to cool down—like your office, your bedroom, or your back porch—take a walk or a jog to cool down and collect your thoughts. I recommend not taking too long to cool off. You do not need six months to cool off! Too much time in silence and separation can lead to total silence and separation.

Perhaps you are dealing with some challenges right now in your relationship, and you are not feeling that true love or love at all. I encourage you to take the time to discuss or address those feelings together. Your love is worth carving out some time to face those challenges head-on. *True love* always has a way of working itself out. So, work it out!

QUESTIONS

What does love mean to you?

_____

_____

_____

_____

In what ways do you express your love to your significant other?

_____

_____

_____

_____

What are some areas where you can improve when it comes to expressing your love to your significant other?

_____

_____

_____

_____

In what ways can you work together to perfect your love for each other?

_____

_____

_____

_____

Trust: Build Trust upon the Truth

Trust and respect are essential in a relationship. You gotta have them! Trust and respect create a special, safe, and secure bond between the two of you. There is nothing like being with someone you can fully trust, confide in, and depend on. A strong and healthy relationship is built on trust, and trust has to be built on the truth. The best way to build trust is through action. Trust, like love, is an action word. You have to prove yourself to be trusted, and that starts with trusting yourself. You have to hold yourself accountable, be committed to being loyal, be committed to being faithful, and be committed to being honest. And when you are honest with yourself, you can be honest with your significant other.

Having trust in your relationship fosters vulnerability. This is a good place to be because it enables you to be open and honest with each other. You feel comfortable with each other, and you can easily (with total confidence) confide in each other. You never want to open up the door of distrust in your relationship. Once you open up the door of distrust, you open up the door for doubt and suspicion, which lead to worry, stress, anxiety, and hurt. You began to worry about if he/she is telling a lie or the truth or what part of their story is the lie or the truth. I know you are familiar with having to tell one lie to cover up another. That first lie can lead to the end of your trust bond with each other. The way to keep that bond of trust in your relationship is to always tell the truth.

SERIOUS TIP

Don't get into the habit of keeping things from each other or lying to each other. Never give your significant other a reason to not trust you. Always be faithful, open, and honest with each other; it will save you a lot of heartache and pain, and it will save the life of your relationship. Once that trust is broken, it is not easy to rebuild, especially if it involves cheating, infidelity or adultery. I am just keeping it real.

NEWS BREAK: ENTITLED—NEVER!

When you are married or in a serious relationship, you NEVER invite someone else into your relationship. Three is definitely a crowd and not allowed! Men, you NEVER have a lady friend closer to you than your significant other. Women, you NEVER have a male friend that is closer to you than your significant other. It is not acceptable! You should NEVER have feelings for someone else or eyes for someone else other than your significant other. You NEVER look at someone else for the purpose of lust. These behaviors are a for-sure way to end your relationship or cause unwanted problems or issues. I encourage you to stay faithful and true to each other and keep your trust bond protected and sacred!

QUESTIONS

How valuable is trust to you in your relationship?

_____

_____

_____

_____

What are some things that you can do personally to assure that your trust bond is never broken?

_____

_____

_____

_____

If your trust bond has been broken, what are some steps that you can take toward rebuilding that trust together?

_____

_____

_____

_____

List three reasons why it is important to always tell the truth.

_____

_____

_____

_____

Communication: It Takes Two!

Communication is another important ingredient in the recipe of love, but it is often missing in the relationship. When that communication piece is missing, it can open the door for misunderstanding, confusion, disagreement, and distance. Some people are not very good at communicating, especially when it comes to expressing their thoughts and feelings. It's okay; I get that. But you have to start somewhere, and you can start by putting that open line of communication into practice! In a relationship, you have to talk to each other and keep that constant flow of communication. It helps you to stay on the same page and meet each other's needs and expectations. Whether you are talking about how each other's days went, what is going on at work, the children, the finances, vacation plans, or the neighbors, it is essential to make communication a priority in your relationship.

COMMERCIAL BREAK

I remember a time when my ex-husband and I would be so angry with each other; we would actually sit down and write out what we were trying to say. This helped us not only to communicate with each other but to hear each other's whole heart, and it kept us from yelling and screaming. At times, it really did work.

When you are having a conversation, it is important to focus on listening and really hearing each other out. When communicating, both of you need to be heard. It's important to listen to each other's thoughts, feelings, opinions, and ideas. Think about this: What both of you have to say matters and should be taken into consideration. It doesn't matter who's right or who's wrong; it's just important that you hear each other out and work together to resolve any issues, problems, or concerns you may have. Even if there aren't any problems or concerns, practice listening to each other; have a conversation and enjoy each other's company.

My heart bleeds when I hear of couples that split up and are clueless as to why. Most of the time, it is because they didn't know how to effectively communicate with each other. Often, when people are asked why they split up or why they got a divorce, their answer is "I don't know." I mean, they are truly questioning what went wrong and why they stopped singing and dancing to their favorite song. Often, we just don't know how to talk to each other. We yell and scream at the top of our lungs instead of talking respectfully and sensibly to each other. We purposely ignore each other, just to get revenge. Or we play the silent game with each other, because we are being selfish or because we've simply chosen not to communicate.

My friend Mrs. Sullivan once shared with me this cute little story about her grandparents, and it clearly illustrates my point. Mrs. Sullivan's grandparents had a long marriage of over fifty years. Her grandmother was the talker, and her grandfather hardly ever spoke at all. There was definitely no communication between the two. One year, they received an electric blanket with dual controls for Christmas. In October, Mrs. Sullivan visited with her family. She had a conversation with her grandfather (when her grandmother was not around), and she found out that he did not like the electric blanket because he was always too hot. Her grandmother, when asked how she liked it, complained that she was always too cold. When Mrs. Sullivan decided to check the blanket for some kind of malfunction, she discovered that their controllers had been reversed for ten months! So, during that whole time, her grandfather had been hot every night because her grandmother kept turning up the heat, but neither one of them had mentioned the problem to each other for ten months straight. This problem could have been easily fixed or resolved if they had just communicated with each other. A lack of communication might not end your marriage, but it will ruin the quality of your life together.

COMMUNICATING IN TRUTH

We've talked about trust and telling the truth, but I want to touch on this very important matter while we are on the subject of communication. It is important that, when you communicate with each other, you *communicate in truth*. Often, when couples communicate with each other, they don't communicate effectively because the truth is not being told. When you are not communicating in truth, neither the conversation nor your relationship will go anywhere. And you will continue to struggle with the same issues or problems.

This is how it will go down: You decide to sit down and have a serious conversation with each other, but you end up scratching your head as you question over and over, "Why isn't this conversation going anywhere?" At some point in the conversation, you begin to think you have lost your mind because something just isn't adding up and nothing seems to make any sense. What is missing here? Perhaps, the truth is missing.

You see, we may communicate with each other, but we will just tell each other what we "think" the other wants to hear or only what we want him/her to know. We believe this will keep the peace and avoid conflict. Yes, for some reason, we don't like conflict. One of my favorite sayings goes like this: 'Avoiding the issue does not void the issue.'" The issues are not going anywhere until they are dealt with. If you keep putting off, avoiding, or withholding the truth, you will continue to go around in circles and never come to any resolution. The conflict will just turn into an emotional roller coaster.

After being with each other for a long time, you become familiar with each other's behaviors and attitudes. So, usually you know when something is wrong. You may not know exactly what it is at times, but you have this gut feeling. When you attempt to ask what is wrong, they respond with "nothing." Or maybe you ask, "How are you doing?" And they respond, "Fine" or "Good" Now, you know something is wrong because of the change in their attitude or behavior, but they insist that nothing is wrong or that they are fine. You eventually come to the conclusion that they are just choosing not to talk about it.

Here is the real deal: When something is on your mind or when something is wrong, you must learn to say, "Sweetheart, there is something wrong, but I don't want to talk about it right now, or I will talk to you about it later." This response gives you peace in knowing that your sweetheart will talk to you about it later. When you learn to do this for each other, it will help you grow in patience and understanding. I know that we live in a microwave generation, and we want all the answers right now! But we have to accept that our partner doesn't want to talk right this minute.

You have to be careful not to push your significant other into talking when they are not ready to talk or when they just need some time and space. I had it bad. I wanted to know right then and there, or else! I learned that this is never a good thing to do. Most times, it ended in an explosive conversation, and you would have thought someone was popping fireworks! You have to respect that they don't want to talk about it right now and trust them to talk to you about it when they are ready. Now, if they take too long to come and talk to you, it is okay to hold them accountable and give them a gentle reminder. The bottom line is to learn to communicate and confide in each other, no matter what is going on.

LISTENING TO EACH OTHER

Remember when your parents used to say "Listen to me when I am talking to you?" Your mother would grab your face (both cheeks with one hand) and turn it toward her to make sure that she had your full attention. Or remember when your teacher would try to get everyone's attention by saying, "I need everyone's undivided attention?" Your parents and your teacher had something important to say, and they wanted to make sure that you were hearing them and that you were listening. If your eyes didn't meet theirs, if there wasn't complete silence in the room while they were talking, then they did not have your full-undivided attention, and this meant that you were not listening.

When communicating with each other, we must make sure that we are listening to what our partners have to say. We often get into the habit of not listening to each other because we are impatiently and anxiously waiting to tell our part of the story. Yeah, we just can't wait to get our two cents in! So, while the other is talking, we are replaying in our minds over and over what we are going to say, hoping that we don't forget it all. We want to get every single word in. When we are not being *good listeners*, we fail to hear what the other person is saying. It's easy to become combative (in silence) while your significant other is speaking. While they are talking, you are thinking, "You got that wrong, that isn't true, that's a lie, etc." So, the question is "How can you hear what your significant other is really trying to say?"

Always give each other the same courtesy and respect; listen (attentively and patiently) to hear each other out. Be sure to give each other time to speak and be sure to listen with your heart. To guide the conversation and move forward to the next best thing, you have to become a good listener. Remember, what both of you have to say is equally important!

QUESTIONS

How important is communication to you in your relationship?

_____

_____

_____

_____

Do you think your relationship lacks communication? Why?

_____

_____

_____

_____

What are some necessary steps you could take to promote effective communication in your relationship?

_____

_____

_____

_____

Compromise: Meet Me in the Middle

When a person is used to being alone and making decisions on their own, it can be difficult for them to understand what it means to compromise in a relationship. In fact, many couples have been in a relationship for several years and still can't agree on one single thing. One wants to do everything their own way, and one disagrees on everything. Compromising in a relationship means that you deny yourself. You see, you now have someone else to consider, and that person is your significant other. This means you shouldn't expect everything to always go your way, and you should be willing to compromise.

Now, you have to learn to consider each other's wants and needs, and sometimes this means considering what is best for both of you. Not only that, but you must consider what is best for your relationship. You will not agree on everything; and no one expects you to agree on everything, but you have to be willing to compromise. You are two different people with different thought patterns, desires, opinions, and ideas. The key is learning to respect and accept each other's differences and learning to make decisions together that will not compromise each other's needs, wants, or happiness. Learning to work together to reach a common goal is a step in the right direction. If you're making a decision on what to cook for dinner, what movie to go see, what restaurant to go eat at, or what family vacation to take, remember that there is a thing called *taking turns*. Just take turns, pull straws, flip a coin, work it out on a calendar or, gentlemen, just be a gentleman and allow the woman to choose first!

Compromising with each other takes some good listening and communication skills. You want to be sure to hear each other out, reason with each other, and discuss the best thing for both of you and/or for the family. A decision should never be settled with "It's my way or the highway." Always remember, it is two of you meeting each other in the middle and making decisions together.

COMMERCIAL BREAK

Never compromise each other's happiness by purposely being difficult or selfish. Selfishness cannot be involved when making decisions together. When you commit to being with someone, you now have someone else's feelings, wants, and needs to consider—there is no room for selfishness. It is *extremely* important to consider your actions and behaviors and how they may affect both of you and your entire family. Learn to be understanding and considerate of each other as you are making decisions together.

You make decisions on just about everything in a relationship—about finances, the family, even the extra butter on the popcorn. We can make decision-making difficult sometimes, especially when neither party is willing to reason with the other. I mean, we really can make a big fuss about putting extra butter on the popcorn—never coming to the conclusion that it can be quite simple. I mean, one of you may like extra butter on your popcorn, and the other may not. To solve this issue, just get two separate bowls, separate the popcorn, and put extra butter on one bowl! Let's hit that easy button together! *That was easy!* Now, on a serious note, there will be tougher decisions you will have to make together, but keep in mind that you are making those decisions with careful consideration and understanding. As you grow, you will learn how to *meet each other in the middle!*

QUESTIONS

What does compromising mean to you in your relationship?

_____

_____

_____

_____

What are some things you consider when compromising with your significant other?

_____

_____

_____

_____

What are some steps you can take in compromising with each other when it comes to making important decisions?

_____

_____

_____

_____

Quality Time: Making Meaningful Memories Together

Quality time is another special ingredient in the recipe of love. Quality time is essential in a relationship. Let me stress this: It's a MUST-HAVE in a relationship! Spending time together is essential because it keeps you close, and it keeps you all up in each other's business. But, seriously, it sustains the life of your relationship. It enables you to stay connected, and it keeps you involved and interested in each other. Genuine, quality time creates those special moments of intimacy. Cuddling, kissing, and holding hands are all ways of communicating with each other, and they are what keep your relationship fresh and alive! Spending quality time together helps you to create and cherish precious and meaningful memories that will last a lifetime!

Now, I am not saying that you need to spend every waking moment together. I believe that it is good and healthy for you and your significant other to have some breathing room or some *me* time. But ask yourself the question "When was the last time I and my significant other went out on a special date or spent some quality time together? Now, if you have to really think about this question, then it's long overdue!

Sometimes, in pursuit of your dreams and goals, you begin to lose the adhesiveness of your relationship bond. In the beginning, you have this special bond, and you are stuck together like glue; nothing can separate you. Then, in all the busyness of life, you both take off running in two different directions, and the adhesiveness starts to separate. Before you know it, you have grown apart.

Life happens, and the workload gets tougher—I get that. I mean, you get married, you have children, and it seems to be *all work and no play.* You get even busier as the kids began to grow up and get involved in extracurricular activities. You take the kids to practice, to sporting games and events, and to other in-school or out-of-school activities, and you come to the conclusion that *there is just not enough time in the day to do anything else.* Now, that's not every couple's story, but perhaps it's your story.

COMMERCIAL BREAK

You have to make the time for each other because, if you are not careful, you will find yourselves living under the same roof but living separate lives. When you don't make the time for each other, your love can slowly start to fizzle out.

I'm sure you have plenty of excuses for avoiding quality time with each other. But enough with all the excuses; it is imperative that you get back to that *QTT*—Quality Time Together! Sometimes, you just have to break away from all the noise and distractions in order to focus on your relationship. It's important to get back to those things that kept you looking all *googly-eyed* at each other. It's essential to get back to those things that kept you engaged with each other. I know you remember the times when you were so mesmerized by each other's presence that you just couldn't take your eyes off each other. Being in each other's presence was all you longed for. Perhaps you need to get back to that puppy love and start barking at each other again. Woof! Woof!

If you are feeling like you don't know what to do together anymore, no worries; my thirty-one-day calendar challenge at the end of the book will give you tons of ideas, along with ways that you can spend *much-needed*, genuine, and meaningful time together!

QUESTIONS

Express what quality time together means to you.

_____

_____

_____

_____

List three reasons why you and your significant other don't spend quality time together.

_____

_____

_____

_____

Look at your reasons for not spending quality time together. What is one thing in your busy schedule that you can sacrifice to spend quality time with each other?

_____

_____

_____

_____

Make It Last Forever

To have a love that will truly last forever, you have to continue doing those things that are going to keep you *together* forever. I strongly encourage you both to stop singing the same old tired song: *we don't have time.* That excuse alone will continue to keep you apart. Don't allow work, the children, your homeboy or homegirl, or anything else keep you from spending that much-needed time alone with each other. You will discover that, somewhere underneath all the busyness and the excuses, your love is still strong, true, and meant to be!

These funny, hilarious quotes and fun and challenging exercises will certainly bring out the kid in you! Causing you to reminisce about the way it used to be, set your hearts ablaze, rekindling the spark and romance you once knew! Get ready to find new, creative, and inspiring ways to keep your love flames burning high! Watch out! Somebody call the fire department!

Sweet-Nothing Quotes

Now, I know these sweet-nothing quotes are going to take you way back to your high school *puppy love* days! It's time to come out of your comfort zone; you have been in for far too long! Get *creative* with these sweet-nothing quotes! I dare you to take a chance on some fun and romance! Don't be afraid to own your romance, all the gooey sappiness included!

Leave these sweet-nothing quotes around the house in places you know your significant other will look or where they get most comfortable—like their favorite chair or recliner, in their underwear or sock drawer, under their pillow, in her vanity, or his man cave. Text or email them to each other; leave them in each other's car. You can even use these sweet-nothing quotes for special occasions, like Valentine's Day or your wedding anniversary and more!

Just when you thought you had no more fun, humor, or romance left in you! Remember, laughter makes the heart grow fonder, and any marriage or relationship can use a good dose of fun, humor, romance, and laughter!

SWEET-NOTHING QUOTES

Like ebony and ivory,
baby, you mean the world to me.

Every time I think of you, I smile,
and your digits I want to dial.

Like ebony and ivory,
with you is where I want to be.

Roses are red, violets are blue,
I can't wait to spend time with you.

Roses are red, violets are blue,
you are a dream come true.

Your smile lights up the world,
so glad you are my girl.

Like ebony and ivory,
baby, we are perfect, can't you see?

Girl, your love is so sweet,
it reminds me of a special treat.

Like ketchup on fries,
You are a beautiful sight to my eyes.

My dream came true
the day I met you.

You light up my life,
so glad that you are my wife.

Like stormy weather,
we flock like birds of a feather.

You treat me like gold,
Our love will never grow old.

Your love is so sweet,
You are my heavenly treat.

Your love is like sugar and spice,
so glad I can call you my wife.

Just like a reality show,
you make it real for me, you know.

Like a hamburger with cheese,
can I take you out please?

Like the Big Dipper in the sky,
I love that sparkle in your eye.

Your smile lights up my world.
so glad you are my girl?

Like the moon in the sky,
your love gets me high.

Your smile lights up a room
can't wait to see you soon.

Roses are red, violets are blue,
and I can't sleep at night thinking of you.

Like beans and cornbread,
girl, I can't get you out of my head.

Can I take you out to eat
and buy you a special treat?

Like ebony and ivory,
with you is where I want to be.

Like ebony and ivory,
you are the only one for me.

Like ketchup on fries,
girl, I will never tell you any lies.

Like the sun shining bright,
I can't wait to take you out tonight.

Like a night out on the town,
sweet love we have found.

Roses are red, violets are blue,
I can't wait to marry you.

Like butter on popcorn,
I know you are the one.

Like a ballpoint pen,
can we start all over again?

Girl, you are such a tease,
you make me weak in the knees.

Like Tropical Punch Kool-Aid,
so glad you are my babe.

Like jelly and peanut butter,
you make my heart flutter.

You are always on my mind.
Will you be my honey, Valentine?

Like a grab bag of cheese puffs,
Your love, I can't get enough.

Like Dutch-chocolate ice-cream,
your love makes me want to scream.

Like a cold and rainy night,
girl, I just want to hold you tight.

The night is still young;
let's go have some fun.

Just like a Mercedes-Benz,
girl I want to take you for a spend.

Just like a river flowing,
Your love keeps me going.

Like a sweet sugar baby,
So glad you are my lady.

One look at you was all it took,
and my whole world shook.

When you came up in my dream,
I knew you would be my queen.

Whenever I call your name,
my heart bursts into flames.

Like a dog named Rover,
I can't wait to come over

I've loved you for a while,
and you still make my heart smile.

When I am feeling down,
I like having you around.

Like a Hershey's chocolate bar,
you are my shining star.

Roses are red, violets are blue,
I'm head over hills for you.

Like raspberry tea,
I will love you for eternity

When all the chips are down,
count on me to be around.

Like reality TV,
you make it real for me.

Like *The Steve Harvey Show*,
oh how I love you so.

Like a winter storm,
I'll keep you safe from harm.

Roses are red, violets are blue,
I'm about to write a love song for you.

Like green grass in the spring,
girl, you make my heart sing.

Like bread and butter,
there will never be another.

Girl, your hair is so pretty,
I want to take you to New York City.

Like a rainbow in the sky,
Your love gets me high.

Your love is so real,
I can't explain how I feel.

When you walk into a room,
my heart goes boom.

Like Cinnamon Toast Crunch,
I love you a whole bunch.

Like biscuits and gravy,
we are good together baby.

Like shopping in a department store,
you are all I need and more.

Like collard greens and cornbread,
I can't get you outta my head.

Like mashed potatoes and gravy,
so glad you are carrying my baby.

Like a sweet potato pie,
you are the apple of my eye.

Like a cold glass of iced tea,
girl, we were meant to be.

Winter, spring, summer, or fall,
honey, you are my all in all.

Like an interesting book,
You make me want to take a second look.

Like a red mustang,
You make my heart sang.

I'm home all alone,
And I miss you when you're gone.

Hickory dickory dock,
you make my heart tic tock.

Like a little red riding boat,
please take me wherever you go.

Like a strawberry smoothie,
you distract me when we're at the movies.

Your love is more than enough,
You got the right stuff.

Like a sticky note,
on my heart, your name I wrote.

Like a good sense of humor,
I am glad our love isn't just a rumor.

Roses are red, violets are blue,
I can't stop thinking about you.

Whether late or on time,
you are always on my mind.

Like a cheeseburger with curly fries,
You're a sight for sore eyes.

Roses are red, violets are blue,
my love for you will forever be true.

Like cruising on *The Love Boat*,
let me buy you a root beer float.

Roses are red, violets are blue,
I give all my love to you.

Like a beauty queen,
you make my heart sing.

Like a full moon,
I can't wait to see you soon.

Like a yellow ribbon around an old tree,
I know you are the right one for me.

Like the moonlight in the sky,
I dig that sparkle in your eye.

Like a tall green apple tree,
with you is where I'd rather be.

Like a lightning bug in the night,
your love light up my life.

Like a good cup of black coffee,
I love it when you are around me.

Like a chocolate ice-cream cone,
I can't wait to take you home.

Like steak sauce on a steak,
I'm gonna take you out on a hot date.

Like white lights on a Christmas tree,
our love shines bright for the world to see.

Like the Easter Rabbit,
you are my bad habit.

From *A* to *Z*,
you are right for me.

Like a bird in a tree,
so glad your love found me.

You plus me
equals eternity.

Roses are red, violets are blue,
I love it when I dream about you.

Roses are red, violets are blue,
you make me feel so brand new.

Like riding a bike,
you know how to hold me just right.

Like flying a kite,
I like the way you hold me tight.

Like the summer heat,
you make my heart skip a beat.

Like french onion dip and chips,
Let's go together on a trip.

Love-in-Action Calendar

Now let's channel that love and romance into some real action! I am one for fun, excitement, and romance! Every day of the week can be ever so sweet when you put your love into *action*. It doesn't have to cost a thing, for the *best* things in life are free! Yes! It's that special four-letter word: *love*. Let's spell this crazy love thing out—it will tell you what this love challenge is all about!

> *L:* Live a little and unwind.
> *O*: Obey your heart and just do it.
> *V*: Venture out and do something that you have never done before.
> *E:* Escape. Getaway from the job, coworkers, kids, neighbors, and friends and go to a bed-and-breakfast every now and again!

I have created a thirty-one-day calendar challenge. This fun, simple, and creative calendar will help you put your love back into action. You don't have to tackle every action every day, but I *challenge* you to give it your best shot!

It's okay to have some fun; it's allowed! Even if you don't feel like it, even if you think that you don't have the time, *and* even if you don't like each other anymore. Be a good sport and just do it anyway! You will be amazed at what a difference this challenge will make in your relationship.

My hope is that this challenge will cause you to develop a habit of doing something together—consistently. Romance is on the horizon! *It's time to live, laugh, and love again!*

Let the Challenge Begin!

DAY 1

Send your significant other a random text and reminisce on a time when you first met: "Do you remember the time when…"

DAY 2

Write one sentence on a sticky note about why you fell in love with your significant other and stick it on the bathroom mirror.

DAY 3

Whoever gets home first—meet your significant other at the door with his/her favorite drink and slippers or socks.

DAY 4

When one spouse is preparing dinner for the night, the other spouse should walk *willingly* and *happily* in the kitchen to help prepare the meal.

DAY 5

Leave your partner's favorite snack beside the bed for him/her.

DAY 6

Watch your favorite movie together.

DAY 7

Write a note of encouragement to your spouse focused on his/her dreams or goals. (You are being supportive.)

DAY 8

Stop by a dollar store and grab a word-search book, coloring book, and crayons (if you don't have these items at home). Before you go to bed, race each other in completing a word search.

DAY 9

Before you go to bed, color in a coloring book together.

DAY 10

Compliment each other on your way out the door.

DAY 11

Start a puzzle. Spend about twenty to twenty-five minutes working on a puzzle together joyfully!

DAY 12

Go out to eat at your favorite fast-food restaurant or do carry out. (Try something new on the menu!)

DAY 13

For about fifteen to twenty minutes, relax in the living room or your bedroom and read a book together. Take turns reading to each other out loud and then discuss what you read together.

DAY 14

Joyfully do a chore for each other that you don't normally do (you do his chore; he does your chore.)

DAY 15

Celebrate that you have made it this far and that you are halfway to the finish line! Take a break and relax and do whatever you feel like doing. If it is nothing, then do absolutely nothing!

DAY 16

Bake a cake together. If you don't bake a cake, bake cookies, brownies, or some other bakery item. (Be in the kitchen baking something together.)

DAY 17

Treat yourself to something sweet together. Enjoy a bowl of your favorite icecream in bed with a movie.

DAY 18

Meet each other for a quick lunch. (Helpful tip: Whoever gets to the restaurant first, order in advance for the sake of time.) Just use the Apps!

DAY 19

Get each other a thank-you card. Write what you are thankful for and leave the cards on each other's pillows. Read them together before you go to bed.

DAY 20

Pull that puzzle out again and work on it for about twenty to twenty-five minutes together with excitement!

DAY 21

For about fifteen to twenty minutes, do some kind of exercise together (go for a walk, stretch, and do some push-ups, sit-ups, squats, etc.) even if you have already worked out for the day.

DAY 22

Pull that word search back out and race at doing a word search together. The winner has bragging rights!

DAY 23

Where is that book you started reading? Read together for about fifteen to twenty minutes before you go to bed and discuss what you read together.

DAY 24

Send each other emails or text messages and discuss dinner for the night. Decide on dinner together (it's about collaborating together.)

DAY 25

Send each other a text message to simply say, "I am thinking of you." (Mean it!)

DAY 26

Get a babysitter (if you have kids), dress up, and go out on a special date.

DAY 27

Find an arts-and-crafts project you can do together. Keep it simple; use your imagination and grab some items from around the house to create and complete your art project.

DAY 28

Stop by the dollar store or a store of your choice and grab something that reminds you of your significant other. Write a sweet note and put it in a cute little bag with the dollar item that you purchased. (Put some thought into it.)

DAY 29

Color in your coloring book together again.

DAY 30

Cook your favorite dinner together. (Men, fix your woman's plate.)

DAY 31

Celebrate that you made it to the finish line! Enjoy your favorite food and drink! Then plan a getaway at a bed-and-breakfast or a hotel. Just get away from your house!

Now give each other a high five or two-thumbs-up because you were committed and dedicated to the challenge. Dance, dance, dance! Put these fun and intimate gestures into practice on a regular basis and take your relationship to new places!

Forever in Love Memory Card Game

This is a simple and fun card game I created that I know you and your significant other will love and enjoy. What do you know, what do you remember, what did you forget, or what new facts will you learn about each other?

There are a total of thirty-six cards in the game, and each card is worth five points, except for the two bonus cards. The two bonus cards are worth ten points each. Cut out the *Forever in Love* cards and feel free to have the cards laminated.

After you have cut out all the cards, you will shuffle them and then turn the cards over on the table—or whatever surface you're using. Then you will take turns turning each card over. You will turn over a card and read the question from the card out loud to your partner, and your partner will answer the question. If they miss the question, you get the five points, and you get to pull another card and repeat the same steps. The one who ends up with the most points wins the game!

The winner gets bragging rights and gets to be pampered by the *one who didn't win* in some special way! Winner's choice! Here are some ideas: The winner may kindly ask you to do some of their chores around the house, cook dinner, or take them out for lunch (whatever their heart desires). Just remember to say please and thank you!

With this fun card game, you just might discover that what you once knew about your significant other has changed, or they may desire different things (for example, instead of regular Coke, you may now like Diet Coke or Dr. Pepper).

A sweet reminder: This game is just for fun, and it's another great opportunity for you to spend some quality time together while you are getting to know each other a little better. Who knows? You might learn something new!

Where did we first meet?

What is my favorite color?

What is my favorite food?

Where was our first date?

What is my favorite restaurant?

What is our anniversary date?

What is my favorite movie?

What is my favorite comedy show?

What is
my favorite
movie
network
channel?

What do I
like to do on
my day off?

What is
my favorite
grocery store
to shop at?

What is my
dream car?

What is my dream vacation?

Where did we go on our honeymoon?

What is my favorite seafood?

What is my first date choice—dinner or a movie?

Would I rather stay at home or go to a sports game?

Would I prefer to read a book or surf the internet?

What's my favorite genre of music?

Which do I like best— cake or pie?

Would I prefer vanilla or chocolate icecream?

Do I prefer socks or barefoot?

Do I prefer a button-down shirt or T-shirt?

Do I prefer reality shows or sitcoms?

Do I prefer to eat dinner in the living room or at the dining room table?

What size shoe do I wear?

Do I like to exercise at home or at the gym?

What is my favorite season?

What is my favorite holiday?

At what age did I get my driver's license?

What school did I attend for college?

What is my favorite animal?

What is my favorite kind of cake?

What is my favorite kind of pie?

Bonus Card: What is my Social Security number?

Bonus Card: What is my driver's license number?

Final Thoughts

The key to a healthy, flourishing, and everlasting relationship is *love*, *hard work*, and *dedication*. I have a T-shirt I made that says "Love Speaks Louder than Words." When you love someone, you show them that you love them in countless ways. It's about putting in the work daily. Yes, it's a daily thing. Look at your regular job. You go to work every day, you work hard, you do your best, and you give it all you got, and the end result is recognition and a paycheck! Showing up and working hard pays off. Giving it your all and doing your best in your relationship will produce great results and it will pay off for a life time!

Remember, it's not always going to be peaches and cream (as we like to say); you will experience some heartache, pain, disappointment, and frustrations, but you have to be willing to deal with all of those things together—with love, understanding, and patience. You live and learn to embrace the hard times and the good times together. You have to be willing to extend grace and show mercy toward each other daily.

In closing, the following things are essential for keeping your relationship healthy and strong: be thankful for what you have, cherish the love you have, value your relationship, take pride in your partnership, appreciate and consider each other, hold each other accountable, and always think of *twenty-one* fun and creative ways to keep your relationship healthy, youthful and alive! Always strive to make each other happy and live at peace with each other.

I hope and pray you both have a beautiful life together filled with lots of love, tons of romance, fun, and excitement, and a special bond that will keep you *forever in love!*

Varinia Peace

Varinia Peace is a woman of God with many gifts and talents—writing, authoring several books, singing, arts and crafts, and making her T-shirts. Creativity should have been her middle name, because she loves to create everything—personalized gifts, gift baskets, birthday cards, her God Cans, T-shirts, and much more. Christ motivates her to encourage and inspire others to pursue their dreams with passion and purpose. She believes that prayer changes things, so she lives by the word of God, which instructs us to pray without ceasing. She is a born entrepreneur who is determined to reach her goals and see her dreams come to pass. She has written several books and songs and also has a few plays and skits under her belt.

Varinia believes that there is more to life than just existing. She knows that we were created for purpose, created for greatness, and she is passionate about doing what she was created to do. One of her greatest passions is people—and leading them to Christ. Her life-long dream is to leave a legacy not only so people will follow but so people will be inspired to live their best lives and leave their mark on this world!

VARINIA'S ACCOMPLISHMENTS

Countless hours of Volunteer Community Service
Founder of Spirit of Peace Gospel Ministry
Founder of His Contagious Joy Ministry
Hosted Gospel Concerts
Guest Speaker at Countless Women's events and functions
Written several books (including four Children's books)
Written many Songs, Jingles, and Quotes
Written several Gospel Plays and Skits
Owns her own Women's Clothing Store
Owns her own T-shirt and Crafts Business: APOP- A Product of
Peace www.aproductofpeace.com